TWO DUDES FROM DAYTONA

A one-act comedy by
Matt Buchanan

Loosely adapted from William Shakespeare's
Two Gentlemen of Verona

www.youthplays.com
info@youthplays.com
424-703-5315

COPYRIGHT RULES TO REMEMBER

CAST OF CHARACTERS

VAL, a young man bound for stardom.

THEO, a young slacker.

SPEED, an enterprising teen.

JULIA, a young Daytona Beach woman.

* LUCY, her friend.

* TANYA, Theo's wealthy mother.

SYLVIA, an up-and-coming leading-lady type.

LANCE, an aging pool boy.

SKIP THURIO, a successful leading-man type.

WILMA DUKE, Silvia's mother and Theo and Skip's agent.

FRANKY, a street kid.

GLORIA, a street kid.

QUEENIE, a street kid.

IRVING, a street kid.

* OTHER STREET KIDS

* MIKE, a car thief.

* BAND OF MUSICIANS

* A BARTENDER

* VARIOUS NEW YORKERS

* VARIOUS OFFICE WORKERS (optional)

* EDDIE MOORE, a cheap private detective.

* One or more POLICE OFFICERS

* Indicates roles that can be easily doubled.

PLAYWRIGHT'S NOTES

Although the characters and story line differ significantly, this play is structured very like the Elizabethan original. For this reason it is very important that only minimal sets be used, so that scene changes can take place more or less instantaneously. Otherwise the rhythm of the play is disrupted. In general, if the specific setting for a particular scene is really important, the characters mention it in the dialogue, so it is not necessary for the set to make the setting clear. Any set dressing should be small enough that the actors themselves can carry it on.

The following characters can be either male or female, though for convenience the male pronoun is used in the stage directions:

Speed
Franky
Other Street Kids
Mike
Band of Musicians
Bartender
New Yorkers
Office Workers
Police Officers

In addition, while they should be played AS male, other characters could probably be played BY girls if necessary.

Costumes can be as over-the-top or as naturalistic as you choose, but they should match. (In other words, if you choose to over-play the surfer looks at the beginning of the play, you should over-play other characters' looks, such as the street kids, Eddie Moore, etc. later on.)

(Daytona Beach. No set is necessary. VAL, in traveling clothes, and THEO, in surfer casual, are saying goodbye.)

VAL: Dude, stop. You're not going to talk me out of it, so stop trying.

THEO: But Daytona Beach won't be the same without you!

VAL: So come with me. The big city awaits. But I know you can't. *(Mocking:)* You're in love.

THEO: I admit it. Julia is in Daytona Beach. So I'm staying.

VAL: Suit yourself, but I think you're crazy. Nothing ever happens here. I'm heading for the Big Apple. Love is for wusses.

THEO: If you're going to call me names...

VAL: I want culture. I want sophistication. Besides, how many famous actors come from Daytona? Broadway, here I come!

THEO: But that's where you and I are different. I like the simple life.

VAL: Don't try to kid me. You like Julia.

THEO: If you were in love, you'd understand.

VAL: Who knows? Maybe I'll meet some hot chick in the big city.

THEO: Well, if you do, I want to hear all about it.

VAL: Count on it, dude.

(They shake hands elaborately and Val exits. After a moment, enter SPEED, rapidly, on his skateboard. He is dressed in skater apparel.)

SPEED: Yo, Theo. Have you seen Val? I've got his plane ticket.

THEO: You just missed him. Did you give my letter to Julia?

SPEED: Oh, I gave it to her. For all the good it did me.

THEO: What did you expect? A tip?

SPEED: Hey, if you two are going to treat me like a messenger boy, it's the least she could do.

THEO: So she sent a reply, then?

SPEED: Did I say that?

THEO: She didn't?

SPEED: I didn't say that either.

> (*Theo takes a semi-playful swipe at Speed, who dodges him easily.*)

THEO: Listen, you little...are you going to tell me what she said?

SPEED: What's it worth to you?

THEO: Oh, fine...here's five bucks.

SPEED: (*Pocketing the bill with a flourish:*) Pleasure doing business with you.

THEO: Now what did she say?

SPEED: Not a thing. Ha!

THEO: Why you little...give me back my five!

SPEED: (*Dodging Theo:*) No way! I did what you paid me for—I told you what she said. It's not my fault she had nothing to say. You know, I don't think you've got much of a shot there, sport.

THEO: Mind your own business.

SPEED: I always do, baby. I always do. Later, dude.

(Speed exits on his board, followed by an exasperated Theo. Enter JULIA and LUCY, in beach cover-ups over swimsuits.)

JULIA: Lucy, what do you think about love?

LUCY: Depends on who you love, I suppose.

JULIA: Well then, who should I love? Who's the cutest boy in Daytona Beach?

LUCY: Well, that's a tall order. Name a few and I'll tell you what I think of them.

JULIA: *(Giggling:)* Well, there's Larry English.

LUCY: Oh, he's cute! And rich, too.

JULIA: I know!

LUCY: But you can do better.

JULIA: Oh. Well, how about Mark Cato?

LUCY: Well, he's rich, too, but that's about all you can say about him.

JULIA: Yeah.

LUCY: I mean, that lisp alone...

JULIA: *(Over-casual:)* Okay...how about Theo?

LUCY: Oh, no! He's a real dork.

JULIA: *(Furious:)* What?!?

LUCY: Ha! I knew it!

JULIA: What?

LUCY: You're in love with Theo!

JULIA: Okay, what if I am? I'm not saying I am, but what if I am? He is not a dork!

LUCY: No, of course not. I was just pulling your leg.

JULIA: He's pretty cute, I guess. But he's never shown the slightest interest in me, so why should I care?

LUCY: Oh, stop! You love him. We both know it. And I know something else. *(Producing a letter:)* Check this out.

JULIA: Where did you get this?

LUCY: From that little punk Speed. I'm pretty sure he was supposed to deliver it to you in person, but you know how he is...always in a hurry.

JULIA: And where did he get it?

LUCY: Duh! From Theo!

JULIA: *(Giving it back. Haughtily:)* Take it back, then. I don't want it. Theo is nothing to me.

LUCY: *(Giving it back again:)* Well, I don't want it either. It's your letter.

JULIA: Fine, then.

(She tears the letter into tiny pieces without reading it, dropping the pieces on the ground.)

If Theo has something to say to me, he can say it to my face, instead of sending notes by teenage hoodlums. What are we, in third grade?

LUCY: If that's the way you want it. Well, I have a lesson with my tennis pro, Alhandro! What a backsi...I mean backhand! See you.

(Lucy flounces off. Julia looks with chagrin at the fallen pieces of paper.)

JULIA: Oh, what did I do that for?

(She picks up a few of the fragments and tries to read them.)

Oh, look! "Lovely Julia." Stupid Julia. *(Tosses it away:)* Oh! "Love-starved Theo!" *(Kisses the paper:)* That goes here—by my heart.

(She puts the fragment in her top and drops to her knees to search the rest.)

Maybe he wrote his name more than once. Here! "Poor, sad Theo!" Oh, don't ever be sad, sweet, sweet Theo! Oh, and here's a big piece! It says here, "Holy Julia." Holy? And here "Passionate Theo." If I fold the paper... *(She does so.)* ...I can put our two names together.

(She puts the folded paper in her top.)

I'd better pick up the rest. Don't want to be a litterbug.

(She carefully gathers up all the fragments and exits. Blackout. Lights up on Theo, reading a letter.)

THEO: Oh, heavenly Julia!

TANYA: *(Off:)* Theo!

(Theo tries hastily to hide the letter as TANYA enters.)

THEO: Oh, hello, Mother.

TANYA: What's that letter you were reading?

THEO: Oh...er...just a letter from Val in New York.

TANYA: Val? What does he say? Let me see the letter.

THEO: Oh, he doesn't really say anything. Just begs me to join him in the city.

TANYA: That's exactly what I wanted to talk to you about.

THEO: *(Uneasy:)* Oh, yes?

TANYA: Oh, yes. I think you should go to the city like Val.

THEO: *(In a panic:)* You want me to be an actor? Why?

TANYA: No, of course I don't want you to be an actor. In fact, I forbid it. But I'm sick of watching you while away your life, bumming around the beach. It's time you made something of yourself. And New York is the place to do it.

THEO: But I am something! And I'm happy here!

TANYA: You're not something a son of mine should be. If you want to keep spending my money and driving my cars, I'm afraid I'm going to have to insist. In fact, I've already scored you a job...the boss owes me a favor. You start tomorrow.

THEO: But, Mother...

TANYA: But me no buts, Theo! You're just going to have to suck it up and give it a try. If you still hate it after three months, you can come home.

THEO: But...

TANYA: This conversation is over, Theo. I suggest you start packing.

> *(She stalks off, leaving Theo looking after her in frustration. Blackout. Lights up on Val and Speed, in New York. Again, no special scenery is needed.)*

VAL: I still don't know what you're doing in New York, Speed. I thought Daytona Beach was your turf.

SPEED: I go where I want. I figure I need a bigger scope for my talents. Besides, you tip better than Theo. Though lately you're just as sickening to be around.

VAL: Oh, that's nice. What are you talking about?

SPEED: You're in love.

VAL: Oh, come on! How do you know that?

SPEED: Please! You've been wandering around Manhattan like a lovesick schoolboy for weeks.

VAL: *(Ruefully:)* That obvious, huh?

SPEED: And you better be careful.

VAL: Why do you say that?

SPEED: Dude, if I can see it, so can other people. And she's your agent's daughter. Crossing Wilma Duke is no way to get a good part.

VAL: I don't know. Maybe Wilma won't care. And living in her house, just think of how many opportunities I'll have to see Sylvia.

SPEED: You're dreaming. Won't care! Wilma Duke is the most powerful agent in New York. She's not going to want her only daughter marrying some bit player.

VAL: Hey!

SPEED: I call 'em like I see 'em. I don't even know how you scored her as an agent. I don't exactly see Broadway beating down your door, sport.

VAL: Give me time! I've only been here a month. Anyway, Sylvia's got her eye on someone else.

SPEED: Oh, yeah?

VAL: She told me so.

SPEED: Oho...so we've progressed to conversation, have we? Instead of just staring at her with your mouth hanging open?

VAL: *(Offended:)* Yes, we have. Last night she had me help her write a love letter to this Don Juan.

SPEED: Who is it?

VAL: She wouldn't tell me. Probably some smarmy leading-man type.

SPEED: I hope you torpedoed the letter.

VAL: I did not. I did the very best I could.

SPEED: Oh, well...it's probably lousy anyway, knowing you.

VAL: Shut up.

SPEED: Don't look now, but here comes the lady herself. Later, dude.

(He exits on his skateboard, as SYLVIA enters. During the following, Speed re-enters quietly and watches.)

SYLVIA: There you are.

VAL: *(Suddenly shy:)* Sylvia! I...erm...I finished your letter. *(Producing it:)* But it was hard to write.

SYLVIA: *(Haughty:)* Well, if it was too much trouble...

VAL: No, no! Anything for you. I was glad to do it. It was just hard.

SYLVIA: *(Suddenly shy:)* And why was that?

VAL: Well, it would have been easier if I had known who it was for.

SYLVIA: Oh. *(Pause.)* Well, I'm still not going to tell you. Thanks, though. *(Taking the letter:)* I'll go send this. *(Teasing:)* And don't you go following me to see where it goes! On second thought, take it back. I guess I don't want it.

(She exits.)

SPEED: Dude, you need help.

VAL: *(Startled:)* I thought you left.

SPEED: I'm here, I'm there, I'm everywhere.

VAL: I wish you were nowhere.

SPEED: Dude, she gave you the perfect opening and you blew it.

VAL: What are you talking about?

SPEED: When she asked you why the letter was hard to write, you should have said, "It gave me pain to write such words of endearment to my rival." I bet that's what she wanted you to say.

VAL: Oh, I can just see myself saying something that wet! And why do you even know words like "endearment?"

SPEED: *(Offended:)* I read! I may be a punk, but I'm not *just* a punk.

VAL: I just don't know how to get her to notice me.

SPEED: You really are as thick as a post, you know that?

VAL: Don't you have someplace to be?

SPEED: Fine. Don't listen to me. But I think it's obvious she *has* noticed you.

VAL: How do you figure?

SPEED: Why else would she give you a love letter?

VAL: She hasn't written me any love letters!

SPEED: Dude, why should she, when she can get you to write 'em yourself? You still don't get it, do you? It's Cyrano de Bergerac in reverse.

VAL: *(Protesting:)* What are you... *(Realizing what Speed said:)*

...Cyrano de Bergerac? The things you know constantly amaze me.

SPEED: Like I said, I read.

VAL: So you're saying this other jerk she loves is me?

SPEED: Jerk is right. Yes, peabrain. She got you to write to yourself. Didn't she hand you the letter?

VAL: *(Light dawns.)* I guess she did.

SPEED: There you go. Come on...it's dinner time. You're buying.

(They exit. Blackout. Lights up on Theo and Julia.)

THEO: Please don't cry. It's only for three months. It will go by fast.

JULIA: It would go by faster if you didn't go.

THEO: I have to. My mother will disown me.

JULIA: So what? If we love each other, what do we need with her money? *(Realizing what she's said:)* Okay, scratch that...we do need her money. I'm not living in a trailer, even for you. But I wish you didn't have to go.

THEO: I'll write all the time. Meanwhile, take this.

(He takes a ring off his finger and presses it into her hand.)

It's my grandfather's ring. Every time you look at it, you can think of me.

JULIA: Then you take mine, too.

(Gives him her ring.)

THEO: I'll wear it over my heart all the time.

TANYA: *(Off:)* Theo!

THEO: Gotta go. *(Kissing her:)* It will feel like an eternity. Wait for me?

JULIA: Always.

(They exit in opposite directions, slowly, without taking their eyes off one another. When they're gone, LANCE enters, looking, as he always does, like Jimmy Buffett on a bad hair day. With him, as always, is CRAB the dog. [If you have one that will behave, a live dog would be fun, but a stuffed one will do.])

LANCE: *(To the audience:)* You know, I think my dog, Crab, is the most unsentimental beast on the face of the earth. When they heard I was moving to New York, the family almost lost it, man. My old lady was crying in her soup. My old man was punching walls and bawling. My sister was inconsolable. So was my brother, the little wuss. But not Crab. Dude, this dog never shed one single tear. Not one. I'll show you how it was:

(Lance begins shedding clothing – nothing risqué – to illustrate his story.)

This flip-flop is my father. No, wait, this one is my mother. No, that can't be right, man. Wait, it is right. Or left. This one has a hole in the sole, so this one is my mother. She never had much soul. This other flip-flop is my father. This belt is my sister. See how skinny she is? She never eats! This hat is my brother. He's always got to be on top of everything. Give himself apoplexy one of these days, man. I am the dog. No, wait...the dog is the dog. *(Pause.)* Then who am I? Oh! I am me, and he is him. Or he. Anyway...

(He does an elaborate puppet show as he narrates.)

Now, here's my old man. *(To the shoe:)* Pops, I'm moving up North. *(As the shoe:)* Oh, boo, hoo, hoo! Oh, no, not our boy! A day I hoped would never come! *(To audience:)* And here's my old lady. *(To the other shoe:)* Ma, I'm going to New York.

(As the shoe:) Ahhh! Oh, nooooooo! Whatever will we do? *(To audience:)* And here's my sister. *(To the belt:)* Sis, I'm off to find my fortune. *(As the belt:)* No, you can't! I'll miss you so! Oh, boo, hoo, hoo! *(To audience:)* And my bro. *(To the hat:)* Bro, I'm done cleaning pools for a living. I'm off to the big city, man. *(As the hat:)* Oh, no! We love you so much! We need you! Don't go! *(To audience:)* And all this time, what does Crab do? He sits there. Not one word does he say, man! No feelings at all. Come on, you unfeeling cur.

> *(Lance exits with Crab. Blackout. Lights up on Val, Sylvia, and SKIP THURIO. Skip is dressed in flamboyant Hollywood movie-idol fashion, complete with Ascot and beret. He is very obviously "chatting up" Sylvia as Val looks on in irritation.)*

SKIP: *(To Sylvia, a hard sell:)* So, yeah, that part really bumped me into star status. I'm a household name these days.

SYLVIA: *(A little irritated by the attention:)* Oh, I'm sure you are.

SKIP: Yep, the girl who finally snags me will be sitting pretty.

SYLVIA: *(To Val:)* Val, you seem sad.

VAL: I do seem sad.

SKIP: *(Sneering:)* Seem? Do you "seem" things you're not?

VAL: Sometimes. So do you.

SKIP: Oh, yes? What do I "seem" that I'm not?

VAL: *(Boldly:)* Smart. Cool.

SKIP: And how can you tell I'm not?

VAL: Well, there's your scarf, for one thing.

SKIP: *(Contemptuously:)* My "scarf" is an Ascot.

VAL: Doesn't make it any less stupid.

SKIP: *(Angry now:)* You want to be careful, my man. I'm a name in this town.

VAL: A stupid name. What kind of name is "Skip?"

SKIP: This from a guy named "Val." Isn't that a girl's name?

SYLVIA: Guys, watch it...here comes Mother.

(The two men assume attitudes of studied casualness as WILMA DUKE enters. She looks every inch the hard-as-nails theatrical agent she is.)

WILMA: Well, Sylvia, you seem to have all the male attention you need for one day. Gentlemen, how are you?

SKIP: In the pink, Wilma, in the pink.

VAL: And me. Any news on a part for me?

WILMA: Be patient, kid. You've only been making the rounds a month.

VAL: I know, I know..."never give up, never give in."

WILMA: That's right. Meanwhile, there's some joker in a suit outside the office looking for you. He looks like a surfer dressed as a banker.

VAL: Theo!

WILMA: I tried to tell him you weren't here, but he seemed to think this is where you could be found. Turns out he was right. Skip, come with me. I need to talk with you privately.

SKIP: The Angelina thing?

WILMA: Privately.

(Wilma ushers Skip off. Val grabs Sylvia excitedly.)

VAL: Theo is here! This is the guy I told you about.

SYLVIA: The one who would have come with you, except he was is love with a girl back in Daytona Beach?

VAL: My best friend, yes. Only his mother made him come anyway. Got him a job in some bank.

(Enter Theo. He does indeed look like a surfer in a suit.)

Theo!

THEO: Val! *(Embracing him:)* And this must be the famous Sylvia.

SYLVIA: I'm not famous yet, despite my mother.

THEO: You are to anyone who's been talking to this guy!

VAL: *(Aside, to Theo:)* Easy, man! *(Aloud:)* I may have told him all about you.

THEO: *(Kissing her hand:)* My lady, your servant.

SYLVIA: *(Giggling:)* I like your friends, Val.

VAL: *(Joking, or pretending to:)* Back off, fella. I saw her first.

SYLVIA: You so didn't. Skip Thurio did, bless his conceited little heart. Well, I'll leave you two to catch up.

(Sylvia exits. Theo and Val embrace again.)

VAL: So, Theo, how's the love of your life?

THEO: Oh, I won't bore you with my story. What about you? I thought love was for wusses!

VAL: *(Laughing:)* Okay, I admit it. I've gone over the wall. Oh, Theo, isn't she fantastic?

THEO: *(Casually:)* Oh, I don't know...she's all right, I guess.

VAL: Don't make me hurt you!

THEO: *(Laughing:)* I'm kidding! She's perfect.

Congratulations.

VAL: Don't congratulate me yet, pal. I think she's just toying with me.

THEO: Is there somebody else?

VAL: Maybe. I can't even tell. Oh, Theo, I can't sleep, I can't eat. She's all I think about!

THEO: My friend, this is payback for making fun of me all those times.

VAL: You got time for some lunch?

THEO: Sorry...unlike some people, I actually have a job.

VAL: Hey! I have a job. Do you think it's easy running from audition to audition all day?

THEO: Anyway, I'm already late for my first day of work. Stay loose. I'll see you later.

(Exit Theo and Val, separately. Enter Lance, with Crab; and Speed, on his skateboard; separately.)

SPEED: Lance! What are you doing here, dude? Has everybody left Daytona Beach?

LANCE: Oh, I thought I'd see what I could make up here. I'm tired of cleaning other people's pools all day, man.

SPEED: All day? Like you ever did a whole day's work in your life!

LANCE: Well, I don't want to become a workaholic.

SPEED: How are things back home?

LANCE: About the same.

SPEED: What about that little gal of Theo's? Julia? Will she wait for him while he's here trying to bust Wall Street?

LANCE: Oh, she'll wait. For a while. A better question is, will he wait for her, man?

SPEED: You got that right. This town is going to eat him alive. And speaking of eating...

LANCE: I know, I know...I'm buying. Come on, then.

(They exit together. Blackout. Lights up on Theo.)

THEO: What am I going to do? If I leave my Julia, I'm a real jerk. If I love Sylvia, I'm twice a jerk. Plus, I'd be doing down my best friend, Val. Three times a jerk. And yet...she's so...New York. So beautiful and sophisticated. She makes Julia look like a hayseed. *(Pause.)* I did love Julia. I did. But it's like I was in love with a twinkling star, and then I saw the sun. It's only Sylvia for me! *(Pause.)* And that makes Val my rival. Well, so be it. For Sylvia's sake I'll betray my friend. And here he comes.

(Enter Val.)

VAL: Theo! My friend! Have you turned the banking world on its ear yet?

THEO: *(Laughing:)* Not yet. But I want to hear about you. How goes the love life?

VAL: I'm glad you asked. Can I tell you a secret?

THEO: I'm all ears, my friend. *(Uncomfortable:)* You know you can trust me.

VAL: She loves me!

THEO: Sylvia? How do you know?

VAL: She told me so! In fact, we're planning on getting married tomorrow night!

THEO: Tomorrow night! So soon?

VAL: Well, when you're in love, why wait?

THEO: And what does her mother think of all this?

VAL: Well, er...that's why it's a secret. We haven't told her. I think she has someone a little more...successful in mind.

THEO: You haven't told her? But won't she be a little annoyed when you come home married?

VAL: Well, yeah...I expect there will be a scene. But Julia thinks it will be easier to ask for forgiveness than to ask for permission. Once Wilma sees that she's got a son-in-law whether she likes it or not, she'll make the best of it. She might even work harder for me.

THEO: How do you figure that?

VAL: Julia thinks if Wilma can't have a son-in-law who's already famous, she'll try to make the one she has famous instead.

THEO: And what about Skip Thurio? Is that an enemy you can afford to make?

VAL: Theo, I don't care! I love Sylvia and she loves me.

THEO: Well, I wish you luck, I really do. Sylvia is a great girl.

VAL: She's the only girl...except for your Julia, of course.

THEO: What? Oh, right. Except for her.

VAL: Well, I'll see you later, Theo. I've got so much to do. Gotta get a license, find a ring...you'll be best man, of course?

THEO: Just tell me where and when.

VAL: I will. Later, dude.

   (Exit Val.)

THEO: *(To Audience:)* Tomorrow night! I've got to work fast!

(Exit Theo. Blackout. Lights up on Julia and Lucy.)

JULIA: It's been weeks and weeks, Lucy!

LUCY: It's been a couple of weeks.

JULIA: It feels longer. Oh, I miss him so much. And I can't stand to think of all the sophisticated New York girls. They're probably all over him!

LUCY: So go to New York to see him. I mean, it's not exactly the sixteenth century. There's this nifty new invention. It's called an airplane.

JULIA: But how can I go see him? I promised I'd wait for him. I promised I'd trust him!

LUCY: So?

JULIA: If I show up in New York he'll know I don't.

LUCY: Don't you?

JULIA: *(Hesitating:)* Well, I do...I do trust him. But I don't trust those New York women. But I don't want him to think I don't trust him.

LUCY: So stay and wait then. What do you want me to say?

JULIA: *(Frustrated:)* Oh, I don't know! If only I could just see him.

LUCY: If you see him, it stands to reason he'll see you.

JULIA: Wait! That's it! I'll go in disguise!

LUCY: As what...a loose New York floozie?

JULIA: *(Still working it out:)* No...I don't want to test him. Just see him. I know! As a boy!

LUCY: Come again?

JULIA: I'll go as an office boy. That will give me an excuse to get close to him without him knowing.

LUCY: If you say so.

JULIA: No, Lucy, it's perfect. Come on...you can help me with my disguise.

(They exit. Blackout. Lights up on Wilma Duke and Skip Thurio.)

WILMA: I'm sorry about this, Skip, but they insist on an audition. It's just a formality.

SKIP: But I'm Skip Thurio! I don't audition! It's an insult!

WILMA: I told them that, but they insisted. And it is a great part. Look...they assured me the part's yours. Just go through the motions.

SKIP: It is a good part. Fine, I'll do it. But I won't like it.

(Exit Skip as Theo enters. Theo gives Skip a dirty look in passing.)

THEO: Er...Ms. Duke?

WILMA: Yes? Who are you? What do you want?

THEO: Er...I'm Val's friend...Theo. Remember?

WILMA: Oh, yes...now I do.

THEO: Do you have a minute?

WILMA: If you really mean a minute, yes.

THEO: What I have to say is very hard for me. Val is my friend.

WILMA: Don't worry about that. He's my client. We're kind of in the same boat.

THEO: *(Not sure how to take this:)* I guess so. Anyway, I just thought you ought to know. It's been worrying me.

WILMA: What has...you've got thirty seconds left.

THEO: It's your daughter, Sylvia.

WILMA: I know, I know. He thinks he's in love with her. Him and half of the actors in town. So?

THEO: She thinks she's in love with him too.

WILMA: That's not so good. Are you sure?

THEO: I'm afraid so. In fact, they're planning to be secretly married...tonight.

WILMA: I see.

THEO: I felt it was my duty to let you know. I love Val, but I think he's making a mistake. Your daughter is far too successful and sophisticated for him.

WILMA: I agree. I've been hoping for some time that she'd take up with someone successful...like Skip Thurio.

THEO: Of course. Or maybe a successful banker or something?

WILMA: *(Considering it:)* Well, yes...there's no rule that says an actress has to marry an actor.

THEO: Exactly. Well, I just thought you should know.

WILMA: And I appreciate it, young man. I really do. If you ever decide to give up banking and tread the boards, you've got an agent.

THEO: Here he comes. Be kind. He is my best friend.

WILMA: Trust me.

　　(Theo exits one way as Val enters another.)

Val! Stop a minute? I want to talk to you.

VAL: Sure, Wilma. Another audition?

WILMA: No, not yet. Patience, kid. No, I want to talk to you about Sylvia.

VAL: *(Nervous:)* Oh?

WILMA: I've noticed you and she have been spending a lot of time together lately.

VAL: We're just friends, honest!

WILMA: No, no, that's not it. I just thought you might know what's going on in her head. I'm worried about her.

VAL: Really?

WILMA: Really. I'm afraid she's falling for that Lothario Skip Thurio.

VAL: Oh.

WILMA: And I think it's a mistake. She's at the beginning of her career. If she hooks up with an established star like Skip she'll always be Skip's wife. I want her to make a name in her own right. Like I did.

VAL: I see.

WILMA: To tell you the truth, I'd been sort of hoping she'd come to like you.

VAL: *(Hopefully:)* Really?

WILMA: Yes. I mean, you're even less well-known than she is.

VAL: *(Ruefully:)* Tell me about it.

WILMA: But as you say, you're just friends. Too bad, but there it is.

VAL: Well, actually...

WILMA: Yes?

VAL: Well, since you put it like that, I guess I can tell you. We're not just friends.

WILMA: Oh?

VAL: In fact, we're engaged.

WILMA: Engaged?

VAL: In fact, we're planning on getting married tonight. We were going to tell you...

WILMA: I knew it! I knew I could trust that young surfer-banker!

VAL: Theo? He told you?

WILMA: He told me all about it. *(Suddenly cold:)* So I suppose you think you've hitched your wagon to a real star, eh?

VAL: What?

WILMA: My services not good enough for you, huh? You thought you'd marry into the profession.

VAL: *(Confused:)* No! What? But you said...

WILMA: Do you really think I'd let my daughter marry a nobody like you?

VAL: But...

WILMA: I know what I said. I was testing you. And it's a good thing I did!

VAL: But I love her!

WILMA: Hah! I can't believe you'd betray me like this! I let you stay in my house, for Pete's sake!

VAL: But...

WILMA: But no more!

VAL: WHAT?

WILMA: I want you out of my house! This instant. But because I like you, I'll give you fifteen minutes to pack.

VAL: I don't care if you throw me out into the street! But don't take my Sylvia from me!

WILMA: If you ever speak to her again, I'll have you killed.

VAL: WHAT?

WILMA: And don't think I can't. I know people.

VAL: Well, go ahead. I can't live without Sylvia anyway! Put out a hit...see if I care!

WILMA: You have ten minutes now. I'd start packing if I were you!

(She storms out. Blackout. Lights up on Lance, with Crab, laboriously writing in a notebook.)

LANCE: *(To himself:)* Okay, pro: she can cook. Con: she never does if she can help it. Pro: her hair is blonde. Con: it would be nice if she had more of it. Pro:...

(Enter Speed, on his skateboard.)

SPEED: Hey, big dude. What're you writing?

LANCE: *(Hastily trying to hide the notebook:)* Nothing, man.

SPEED: It didn't look like nothing. I didn't even know you could write. Let me see.

LANCE: It's private, man!

SPEED: *(Snatching the notebook:)* Why else would I want to read it? *(Reading:)* "Pro: she's pretty smart. Con: she's smarter than me. Pro:" *(To Lance:)* What is this...a shopping list?

LANCE: If you must know, man, I've met a lady, and I'm trying to decide what to do about it.

SPEED: Dude, if you don't know that, I can't help you.

LANCE: Hey, man, I don't remember asking for any help.

SPEED: Well, what's the problem?

LANCE: She won't leave me alone! I'm not so sure I'm down with that, man.

SPEED: *(Reading:)* "Pro: she likes me." *(To Lance:)* Well, that in itself ought to seal the deal. How often does that happen? *(Reading:)* Con: she likes everybody." *(To Lance:)* Well, that could be a problem...

LANCE: *(Snatching back the notebook:)* Give me that! So, you heard Val is out on the street?

SPEED: It'll be good for him. Too much luxury is dangerous.

LANCE: Too much work is dangerous, man. That's my philosophy.

SPEED: *(Ironically:)* Good you came to New York, then. Nobody works too hard here.

LANCE: I worry about Val, though. He's not as tough as you and me, man.

SPEED: Let's go look for him. I hope he's not going near any bridges.

LANCE: Lead, and I'll follow. But watch the pace. I don't like to sweat, man.

(They exit. Blackout. Lights up on Wilma Duke, Skip Thurio and Theo.)

WILMA: Don't worry, Skip. Now that that snake in my bosom is out of the picture, Sylvia will come to see what's good for her.

SKIP: It doesn't look like it to me. All she does is storm around cursing you and crying for Val.

WILMA: Give it a little time. Theo, you agree?

THEO: Well, I do, but—

WILMA: But?

THEO: Well, we might hurry it along. If I could have some time to work on her—

SKIP: Wait a minute—

WILMA: No, Skip, I think I see where he's going.

THEO: If I could speak with her alone, I feel sure I could convince her it's foolish to keep on after Val. After all, no one knows him better than I do. Who better to tell her why he's not worthy of her?

SKIP: Okay, granted, but just because she stops loving Val doesn't mean she'll start loving me.

THEO: Well, so I can work on that, too. I'll tell her all your virtues. Er...what are they, by the way? I assume you have some?

SKIP: What's that supposed to mean?

THEO: Nothing, nothing! But Skip, you need to work harder too. You may think you're a good catch...

SKIP: Again, with the insults...

THEO: ...but you can't trust to that. You have to really go after her. Pull out all the stops.

SKIP: What do you mean?

THEO: You need to show her how much you love her. Sing under her window. Write her poetry...

SKIP: Poetry?!

THEO: Send her flowers. Anything you can think of.

SKIP: I could buy her a car!

THEO: Let's not get carried away. No, on second thought, why not? Good idea.

SKIP: Well, I'll take your advice. But you will tell her about me as well?

THEO: Count on it.

SKIP: I was wrong about you, Theo. You're all right.

WILMA: That's settled, then. Skip, come with me. I want to talk about that audition.

(Wilma and Skip exit.)

THEO: Perfect! That's Skip out of the way. He's sure to make a blithering idiot of himself, and she'll hate it. Now to see if I can sell me.

(Exit. Blackout. Lights up on Val, Speed, Lance, and a collection of colorful STREET KIDS. [Note: it is very important that these kids not feel like a real "gang" in the gun-toting, drug-selling sense of the word, and also that they not represent ethnic stereotypes. They are basically innocent kids playing at being tougher than they are.] Among them are FRANKY, GLORIA, QUEENIE and IRVING. The Street Kids surround the three non-New Yorkers.)

SPEED: Let me do all the talking.

FRANKY: You three look like you're lost.

SPEED: No, no. Not lost. How's everybody doing?

GLORIA: We're doing great.

IRVING: *You* might not be.

   (A few Street Kids laugh.)

SPEED: We don't want any trouble, friends.

QUEENIE: Oh, so now we're your friends. When did that happen?

   (More laughter, nods of agreement, a few "yeahs.")

LANCE: Hey, dudes...every man is my friend, man.

QUEENIE: Just the men?

SPEED: *(Aside, simultaneously:)* I said let me do the talking!

FRANKY: What are you doing in our neighborhood, *("Air quotes:")* "friends?"

VAL: Looking for a place to stay. I got kicked out of my house.

FRANKY: Awe, that's sad. *(To other Street Kids:)* Isn't that sad?

   (Murmurs of sarcastic agreement.)

GLORIA: Why?

VAL: Well, see, I fell in love with my agent's daughter, and...

   (Speed elbows him hard in the ribs.)

...Er—I mean...I killed a man!

   (The Street Kids make various impressed noises—"Oooh!" "Wow!" etc.)

In a fair fight, of course.

LANCE: It's true. I saw it.

QUEENIE: Maybe you guys are cool.

VAL: We are. Very cool.

FRANKY: Okay, then. How about joining our gang?

SPEED: I don't know about this...

VAL: It would be an honor.

LANCE: *(Aside, to Val:)* Dude, are you sure? They're kids, man!

VAL: *(Aside, to Lance:)* Who probably know the city better than anyone. Certainly better than us. *(To Street Kids:)* Lead the way to the initiation!

EDDIE: Follow us.

(They exit. Enter Skip Thurio, very nervous. He moves center stage and looks around, to no avail. He checks his watch. He paces. Finally MIKE strolls up to him from behind, making him jump.)

MIKE: Are you Thurio?

SKIP: Oh! I mean...yes. Sorry, you startled me. I wasn't scared...just startled.

MIKE: Glad to know that, champ. You got the dough?

SKIP: *(Patting his breast pocket:)* Yes. You're sure she'll like it?

MIKE: Trust me...it can't lose. The car's a classic. Candy apple red and all.

SKIP: Okay. *(Handing him an envelope:)* It's all there, I assure you.

MIKE: *(Counting:)* Oh, I trust you. I just like to be sure. *(Finishing the count:)* Okay, sport.

SKIP: Now you have the address for delivery, right? Wilma Duke's house?

MIKE: Gotcha. Pleasure doing business with you.

SKIP: Er...likewise.

> *(They exit, separately. Blackout. Lights up on a Band of MUSICIANS, ineffectively hiding. [Use your imagination. They could be hiding behind potted plants, a bench, anything.] They could be dressed as anything from tuxedo-wearing soul singers to Mariachis, and may or may not have instruments. Enter Skip Thurio, leading Sylvia.)*

SYLVIA: Skip, just a tip for future reference. If you're going to give a girl a car, try and get one that's not stolen. I've never been so embarrassed in my life as when that cop pulled me over and handcuffed me.

SKIP: Yes, well, I'm very sorry about that, Sylvia. This will make up for it.

SYLVIA: What is all this anyway? You're very mysterious.

SKIP: Almost there.

> *(Skip stops, turns to face Sylvia, and takes both her hands in his.)*

Sylvia, there's something I've been meaning to say to you for a long time.

SYLVIA: *(Aside:)* Oh, no!

SKIP: Sylvia, I...well, I thought of the perfect way to tell you how I feel. Listen:

> *("Listen" was their cue, but the Musicians have been silently bickering amongst themselves and miss it.)*

(Louder:) Listen!

SYLVIA: I'm listening. What did you want to say?

SKIP: No, no! LISTEN!

> *(One of the Musicians nudges the others, and with much pushing and shoving [and noise] they emerge from their hiding place and burst into song. The song can be sung to the tune of "Twinkle, Twinkle, Little Star," or to any other tune that fits, or even sort of fits.)*

MUSICIANS: LOVELY, LOVELY SYLVIA!
WHEN SHE FROWNS IT KILLS ME, AH!
WHEN SHE SMILES AT ME I AM
JUST AS HAPPY AS A CLAM!
LOVELY, LOVELY SYLVIA!
HOW I LOVE MY SYLVIA!

SYLVIA: *(Appalled:)* Oh, Skip, no!

SKIP: I wrote the words myself.

SYLVIA: They're truly awful, Skip!

SKIP: Well, you try rhyming with "Sylvia." All I could think of was "diarrhea."

MUSICIANS: LOVELY SYLVIA'S SMALLEST WISH
IS TO ME MY FONDEST ITCH!
WHAT SHE HATES I ALSO HATE!
SYLVIA, SYLVIA, YOU'RE SO GREAT!
LOVELY, LOVELY SYLVIA!
HOW I LOVE MY SIL...VI...A!

> *(Sylvia finally gives up the struggle and falls out laughing, to Skip's extreme chagrin.)*

SYLVIA: Oh, Skip! How perfectly ridiculous!

SKIP: You didn't like it? I wrote it myself!

SYLVIA: *(Still laughing:)* Even more perfect! Oh, Skip, thank you! I haven't laughed like this in ages. Not since Val went away! You poor idiot, thank you!

(She rushes off, stifling still more laughter. Skip stares after her, crestfallen. The Musicians have stopped and stand expectantly. Finally, one of them gets up the courage to approach Skip, hand out for payment. Skip looks at him and barks — literally barks — viciously at him. The Musicians make a hasty exit, leaving Skip alone. Blackout. Lights up on Theo and Sylvia.)

THEO: I can't help it, Sylvia! You're all I think about.

SYLVIA: Tell me why. But don't pull a Skip Thurio.

THEO: All right.

(Skip Thurio enters, unseen by them. He stops when he sees them, and stands too far away to clearly hear what they're saying, but not too far to see the obvious body language.)

You're the most beautiful girl I've ever seen. That's for starters.

SYLVIA: Okay. What else?

THEO: And you're so sophisticated and elegant! Oh, Sylvia, I love you so!

SKIP: Aha!

THEO: Skip!

SYLVIA: Skip! What do you want now?

SKIP: *(Ignoring her. To Theo:)* I knew I couldn't trust you! Put 'em up!

(Skip adopts a ridiculous 1910-era boxing pose.)

THEO: No, no, Skip! You've got it all wrong!

SKIP: I don't think so! Come on, defend yourself.

JULIA: Skip, stop acting like a child!

THEO: *(Holding up his hands in peace:)* You're making a mistake, my friend. *(To Sylvia:)* Would you excuse us a moment, Sylvia?

SYLVIA: Oh, you're both such...boys!

(She exits.)

THEO: Put down your dukes, Skip. I'm your friend.

SKIP: I know what I saw! You were flirting with her!

THEO: Of course I was.

SKIP: So you admit it?!

THEO: For you, Skip. I was flirting on your behalf!

SKIP: What?

THEO: You don't think I was trying to win her for myself?

SKIP: Yes I do!

THEO: I wouldn't do that to you.

SKIP: I heard you call her elegant. I heard you say "I love you!" I warn you, Theo, I'm no gentleman. If you won't defend yourself I'll beat you anyway!

THEO: Of course I said those things! As you! I was telling her what *you* feel, not what I feel!

SKIP: Oh?

THEO: I told her you were too shy to tell her how you feel.

SKIP: How is that being my friend? Telling the girl I love that I'm shy? I'm not shy!

THEO: Yes you are...or you'd better be. After that performance the other night, what else could I say?

SKIP: Huh?

THEO: I told her all that was just because you're too shy to talk to her.

SKIP: I still don't know where you get off telling her I'm shy!

THEO: Look...would you rather she thinks you're shy, or an idiot? Because I have to tell you, that's where she was going.

SKIP: Really?

THEO: Besides, girls like shy guys. They think they're deep and sensitive.

SKIP: They do?

THEO: Believe me, you'll thank me later. Now go away and let me work on her.

SKIP: *(Still doubtful:)* Okay...if you say so.

(Exit Skip. Theo checks his breath on the back of his hand and calls off.)

THEO: Oh, Sylvia? Where were we?

(Exit Theo. Blackout. Lights up on Julia, dressed as an office boy, and a BARTENDER. There may be a few small tables or stools to indicate a bar or restaurant. In another part of the stage, Theo, Sylvia, and a few other New Yorkers carouse in the background.)

BARTENDER: Sure, I know Theo. Comes in here all the time. I think he's in the back now.

JULIA: Can you take me to him? I've...er...I've got some important papers for him to sign.

BARTENDER: Sure...though I think he might be a little busy.

JULIA: Busy? What do you mean?

BARTENDER: You'll see.

(He leads her to the other side of the stage, where we can now hear the conversation between Theo and Sylvia. Julia stands and listens with the Bartender, unnoticed by the others.)

THEO: I don't know why you don't believe me.

SYLVIA: Maybe it's because I know for a fact that you're a cheater and a liar.

THEO: How can you say that?

SYLVIA: Aren't you the same guy who was so in love that you didn't want to leave Daytona?

THEO: Oh, that.

SYLVIA: Yes, that. How are you in love with me if you're in love with her?

THEO: That's totally different! Julia's a great girl...the best!...but that was just a fling.

JULIA: Oh!

SYLVIA: A fling?

THEO: An infatuation. Julia is nothing compared to you. She's a small-town girl. You're sophisticated and elegant and perfect.

BARTENDER: What's the matter, young feller? You don't look so hot.

JULIA: I'm fine. Just a little faint. Er...I think I'm coming down with something.

THEO: How can you think I could even look at Julia now that I've met you?

JULIA: Oh!

BARTENDER: Maybe you'd better sit down. Let me take you over here.

(He takes to take her to a table near Theo and Sylvia.)

JULIA: No! I'll go home. Thank you...I'll be fine.

(Julia runs off. Blackout. Lights up on Lance, with Crab.)

LANCE: *(To audience:)* Man's best friend, my left elbow! You want to talk about ungrateful? I brought Crab up from a puppy, man! I saved him from drowning when four or five of his brothers and sisters perished! And this is how he pays me back. *(To Crab:)* Man, are you a hard one to live with! *(To audience:)* It's bad enough when he misbehaves, but when I am punished for it...man, it's too much. So we're all settling down for the night...those are some righteous kids once you get to know them...when there's this awful smell. Of course I knew what it was right away. I'm sorry to say I've smelled it before. But then everybody's looking at *me*! I tired to tell them, but nooooo... *(To Crab:)* What have you been eating when I wasn't looking, you ungrateful beast, huh? *(To audience:)* They kicked me out of the hideout! Now where am I going to sleep, man? Ah, well, it's a dog's life.

(He shuffles off dejectedly. Blackout. Lights up on Theo at work. There may be a desk or two, and possibly some other Office Workers about. Enter Julia, still dressed as an office boy.)

JULIA: *(Putting on a deep voice:)* Any messages, sir?

THEO: What? Oh. You're new, aren't you? These office boys never last long. What's your name, kid?

JULIA: Sebastian, sir.

THEO: Well, Sebastian, as it happens I do have an errand for you. I want...say, haven't I seen you someplace before?

JULIA: Er...I don't think so, sir.

THEO: You look familiar. Well, be that as it may. Can I trust you on a delicate mission?

JULIA: I think so, sir.

THEO: Good. You know that actress, Sylvia Duke? She was in here last week.

JULIA: I think so, sir.

THEO: She lives with her mother. That's Wilma Duke, the famous agent. You know where that is?

JULIA: Yes, sir. Doesn't everyone?

THEO: Good.

(He removes the ring from his finger. Julia gasps.)

What's the matter, kid?

JULIA: Nothing, sir.

THEO: Good. Now, I want you to take this ring and deliver it to Sylvia.

JULIA: *(Choking back tears:)* Yes, sir.

THEO: Now, don't lose it! The girl who gave that to me loved me very much. And now I'm giving it to Sylvia. Why are you crying, kid?

JULIA: *(Through tears:)* I can't help it, sir. I can't help feeling sorry for the girl.

THEO: What girl...Sylvia?

JULIA: No, Juli...er, the girl who gave you that ring.

THEO: Julia? Why should you feel sorry for her?

JULIA: Well, sir, she must have loved you very much to have given you that ring. As much as you love Sylvia.

THEO: Julia was a good kid.

JULIA: Was? So she's dead, then?

THEO: What? No, not as far as I know. Why?

JULIA: It just makes me sad to think of her, sitting at home waiting for you. Of her thinking you love her as she loves you...thinking you're not a cheater and a louse...not knowing the truth.

THEO: Hey, hey! Let's have less of that! You just take this ring to Sylvia like I ask! I love her like crazy, and I think this may just turn the tide.

JULIA: *(Swallowing hard:)* Yes, sir.

THEO: And let me know what she says!

(Julia starts to exit with the ring. Theo calls after her.)

And see if she'll give you a picture! I want to look at her on my desk every day!

(Julia exits with a loud sob. Blackout. Lights up on Sylvia and EDDIE MOORE, who looks like what he is...a shoddy private eye.)

SYLVIA: You're sure you're up for this job?

EDDIE: Never you worry. I been doing this kinda work since you was in diapers, pardon my Swedish. There ain't much about finding lost people that Eddie Moore don't know.

SYLVIA: It's very important to me.

EDDIE: If this guy's in the city, old Eddie will find him.

SYLVIA: My mother threw him out of the house, and I don't know where he's gone, but he can't have got far. I love him dearly, but he's not too street-smart.

EDDIE: You got a pitcher?

SYLVIA: I brought his head shot. *(Handing it over:)* He might not look quite so put together anymore.

EDDIE: Don't you worry about that. He could be disguised as the Queen of England and Eddie Moore would find him.

SYLVIA: I'm counting on you.

EDDIE: Now, I get a hundred a day, plus expenses.

SYLVIA: I know. I've brought your first week's money. *(Handing it over:)* And an extra five hundred if you find him.

EDDIE: *When* I find him, sweetheart. *When* I find him.

SYLVIA: You have my number. Let me know when you know something.

EDDIE: Count on it, sister.

(*They shake hands, and Eddie slinks off. Enter Julia.*)

JULIA: Excuse me...is your name Sylvia?

SYLVIA: It is. Who wants to know?

JULIA: I have a message for you from Theo.

SYLVIA: Oh, no!

JULIA: Ma'am?

SYLVIA: I want no message from that rat.

JULIA: He asked for your picture, ma'am. And he sent you this ring.

(*She tries to hand Sylvia the ring, but Sylvia won't take it.*)

SYLVIA: Well, I suppose he's welcome to a picture. Any fan gets one. I'll even sign it. Tell him it'll be delivered to his office in the morning.

JULIA: Yes, ma'am.

SYLVIA: But tell him this, too: he'd do better to decorate his office with another girl's picture instead of mine. One named Julia.

JULIA: Oh!

SYLVIA: What?

JULIA: Nothing. But what about this ring? He'll be mad if I come back with it. Won't you take it?

SYLVIA: I know that ring. He's told me a hundred times...his first love, Julia, gave it to him. I will not do her the disservice of taking it. Sisterhood means something, even if you can't understand it.

JULIA: She thanks you, ma'am.

SYLVIA: What's that?

JULIA: I mean, I thank you for caring so much about poor Julia.

SYLVIA: What, do you know her?

JULIA: Almost as well as I know myself. When I think about how he's wronged her I can't help crying, even though I'm a boy.

SYLVIA: Does she know he's betraying her like this?

JULIA: I think she suspects it, ma'am.

SYLVIA: Tell me...is she pretty, this Julia?

JULIA: She's not as pretty as she was, to tell you the truth.

SYLVIA: How sad!

JULIA: No offense, but I think when she thought Theo loved her, she was as pretty as you, ma'am. Maybe not as sophisticated, but just as pretty.

SYLVIA: How tall is she?

JULIA: Oh, about as tall as I am. She looks a lot like me, in fact. If she were a boy, I mean.

SYLVIA: Well, I won't take her ring. But here...take a tip anyway. It's not your fault you work for a louse.

(Sylvia hands Julia some money and exits. Julia looks after her.)

JULIA: *(To audience:)* Oh! I knew she'd be pretty, but I wish she weren't so nice. It would make her easier to hate for calling my Theo a louse. Even if he is one!

(Blackout. Lights up on Theo and Skip Thurio.)

SKIP: I just don't understand it. She still doesn't seem to love me. I think there must be someone else.

THEO: *(Nervous:)* Of course there's someone else, you poor fish! Val!

SKIP: No, no. It can't be him. I told her he doesn't love her anymore.

THEO: And she believed you?

SKIP: Well, you know...Wilma threw him out, so he wasn't there to contradict me. God knows where he's gotten to. I told her I saw him in some dive, hitting on every girl in the place.

THEO: Well, that sounds excellent.

SKIP: But she still won't go for me. I need advice, Theo.

THEO: Are you still playing it shy?

SKIP: After you fed her that story, what choice do I have?

THEO: Well, that should work. Let me think about it and get back to you.

SKIP: All right, but don't take too long. I still think there's someone else.

(Exit Skip. Enter Julia.)

THEO: Ah, Sebastian. Did you give her the ring? Was she pleased? Tell me what she said!

JULIA: Pleased? No. In fact, she sent the ring back again. Here it is.

THEO: Keep it. I don't want it.

JULIA: Oh!

THEO: What's the matter?

JULIA: Nothing. She did say she'd send you a signed picture.

THEO: Well, that's something.

JULIA: But she said you'd be better to decorate your office with Julia's picture.

THEO: Still, she sent it, right? I'm making progress. Come on, Sebastian. I like you. I don't know why, but I do. Let's go get some dinner, you and I.

(Exit Theo.)

JULIA: I'll follow you anywhere, Theo. If I can't have you as Julia, at least I can have you as Sebastian.

(Exit Julia, following Theo. Blackout. Lights up on Sylvia and Eddie Moore. Sylvia is dressed down and wearing sunglasses, though it is evening.)

EDDIE: I still think this is a mistake, sister. Eddie Moore works better alone.

SYLVIA: Well, in case you haven't noticed, Eddie, I don't trust you. It's been a week, and you haven't found Val.

EDDIE: Hey, it's a big city.

SYLVIA: Be that as it may, Eddie, I'm coming with you. I want to see just how you're spending my money.

EDDIE: Suit yourself, but this ain't the safest part of town. I can't be held responsible.

FRANKY: *(Entering:)* Well, well, well! What have we here?

GLORIA: *(Entering:)* They look lost to me, Franky.

IRVING: *(Entering:)* Yeah, they do, Gloria. Don't they, Franky?

> *(Queenie and the rest of the Street Kids enter. They surround Sylvia and Eddie.)*

QUEENIE: You folks lost?

EDDIE: *(Aside, to Sylvia:)* Let me do the talking.

SYLVIA: *(Aside, to Eddie:)* Oh, shut up! *(To Street Kids:)* No, we're not lost, kids. But thanks for asking.

FRANKY: Well, if you're not lost, you're trespassing on purpose.

QUEENIE: Yeah. This is our turf.

IRVING: I think we should take 'em to see Ace.

SYLVIA: Ace? Who's Ace?

GLORIA: He's our new leader.

IRVING: He killed a guy once.

EDDIE: I think this is where Eddie Moore gets off. *(Looking off:)* Is that a cop?

> *(The Street Kids look where he's looking, and he dashes off. They realize they've been had, but don't give chase.)*

FRANKY: Never mind. A bird in the hand. Come on, sister. We're taking you to Ace.

SYLVIA: *(Not remotely frightened:)* Tell me about this "Ace." Where does he come from?

GLORIA: We don't know. He just showed up one day a week or so ago, with Speed and Lance.

IRVING: But we had to let Lance go.

QUEENIE: The guy had a serious gas issue.

IRVING: Terrible.

SYLVIA: *(Giggling:)* Well, okay, then. I guess I'm your prisoner. Might as well get it over with. Take me to Ace.

> *(They exit. Blackout. Lights up on Theo and Julia, still dressed as Sebastian.)*

THEO: Sebastian, there you are! I need your help!

JULIA: What can I do for you, sir?

THEO: Well, for a start, you can quit calling me sir. My name's Theo.

JULIA: Okay. Theo.

THEO: I like you, kid. I don't know why. I feel like I can trust you.

JULIA: *(Aside:)* To the ends of the earth!

THEO: There's just something about you. You're sure we never met before last week?

JULIA: I can promise you you've never set eyes on Sebastian before that.

THEO: It's very strange. I feel like I've known you forever. Anyway, I need your help.

JULIA: Anything, Theo.

THEO: It's Sylvia. She's disappeared.

JULIA: How awful!

THEO: She went off to look for that idiot she thinks she's in love with...Val, isn't it?

JULIA: Your best friend, Val?

THEO: How do you know that? Never mind. Yes, that's the one. Ever since her mother threw him out he's been lord-only-knows where.

JULIA: And she went to look for him?

THEO: *(Nodding:)* Hired a private detective, but he ran out on her. I caught up with him and threw a scare into him...wasn't too hard, to be honest...and I got out of him that she's been kidnapped.

JULIA: *(Genuinely concerned:)* Kidnapped?

THEO: By a gang of street kids or something. And this clown she hired just ran off and left her with them.

JULIA: What are you going to do?

THEO: We. You and me.

JULIA: I'll do what I can, but what can we do?

THEO: We can rescue her, of course. If that doesn't show her I'm the better man, I don't know what will.

JULIA: Oh, I know you are! *(Aside:)* If you only knew!

THEO: I mean, I can't imagine Val coming to her rescue. He wouldn't know what to do with himself on the streets. Totally clueless.

JULIA: But how?

THEO: Well, that idiot private eye told me about where they met this vicious gang. We'll start there. Can you use your fists?

JULIA: *(Sadly:)* No. I'm afraid I'm not much of a man.

THEO: Never mind. You can come along for moral support. I don't know why, but you give me confidence in myself. Come on.

(They exit. Enter Skip Thurio and Lance, with Crab, from opposite directions.)

LANCE: Hey, aren't you that guy?

SKIP: *(Haughty:)* What? To what guy are you referring?

LANCE: You know...the guy. In the thing.

SKIP: From which hospital have you escaped?

LANCE: In the movie! That guy in the movie! Aren't you him, man?

SKIP: *(Relaxing:)* Oh! Yes, I am he. I suppose you want an autograph?

LANCE: I'd rather have a burrito, but if that's all you got, man...

SKIP: Say, do you know your way around this place?

LANCE: Better than you, I bet.

SKIP: I'm looking for a girl.

LANCE: Hey man, I can't help you there! What do I look like?

SKIP: *(Irritated:)* No, no...a particular girl.　She's been kidnapped by a heinous gang of thugs.

LANCE: That's awful, man!

SKIP: She was with a private investigator of sorts, but he was able to affect a valiant escape.　Or so he told me...after I paid him off, naturally.

LANCE: *(Scenting money:)* Naturally.

SKIP: Anyway...say, do you smell something?

LANCE: *(Glaring reproachfully at Crab:)* Don't look at me, man!

SKIP: Anyway, apparently this gang was taking her to their leader...some ruffian named "Ace."

LANCE: Hey!　I know those dudes, man!

SKIP: Are you sure?

LANCE: Absolutely.

SKIP: Can you take me to them?

LANCE: Well sure, man...but as long as you're paying people off...

SKIP: Don't you worry.　I'll make it worth your while.

LANCE: Well, okay, then.　Follow me, man.

> *(They exit, preferably in the opposite direction from that taken by Theo and Julia.　Blackout.　Lights up on the hideout of the Street Kids.　Val, Speed and a few Street Kids are playing cards.　Enter the rest of the Street Kids, with Sylvia in tow.)*

FRANKY: Yo, Ace!　We brought you a prisoner!

GLORIA: She was trespassing on our territory!

IRVING: Make an example of her, Ace!

VAL: Sylvia!

SYLVIA: Val!

QUEENIE: Val?

FRANKY: Your name is Val?

VAL: Yes, well...

SYLVIA: I've been looking everywhere for you! *(They embrace, to the disgust of the Street Kids:)*

QUEENIE: You know this broad?

IRVING: I would think that was obvious.

VAL: Of course! Guys, this is Sylvia! The girl I told you about. Her mom threw me out.

FRANKY: You said you killed a guy!

SYLVIA: What?

GLORIA: That's right! You said that!

VAL: No, no...er...I meant, I killed 'em in the audience! I killed 'em with my performance!

IRVING: Lame!

SYLVIA: You almost killed me when you left.

VAL: Me too. How did you ever find me?

SYLVIA: I didn't. These kids found me.

VAL: Well, however it happened, I'm glad.

FRANKY: Can you two knock off the sappy stuff? We're still here, you know.

QUEENIE: Yeah...sensitive ears, and all that!

VAL: Oh, shut up!

IRVING: There is that outlook, of course...

(Theo and Julia rush in.)

THEO: Stand and fight, you ruffians!

JULIA: Yeah! Stand and fight!

THEO: Release the lady or I'll make you!

SYLVIA: But, wait...

VAL: *(Simultaneously:)* Theo!

FRANKY: *(Simultaneously:)* Never!

(Big, comic fight, involving as much tumbling and other comic stage combat as your cast can manage. Val and Sylvia stand back and watch, but Speed participates with gusto, and if the skateboard can be worked in, so much the better. At the end of the chaos, Theo and Julia are subdued, and stand surrounded by Street Kids.)

GLORIA: What shall we do with them, Ace, huh?

FRANKY: Never mind him! He's a fake. I'm the boss again.

IRVING: Since when were you the boss?

THEO: Wait a minute! Look, we admit we're beaten.

JULIA: You fought heroically though, Theo.

THEO: Thanks, Sebastian. But I know when I'm outnumbered. Listen...I'll pay you to let us go. I'm a banker.

FRANKY: Well, that sounds okay. Fork over the cash!

THEO: Er...I don't actually have it on me. But you can trust me!

JULIA: He's very trustworthy...except in one area!

QUEENIE: Cash only! Let's kill 'em!

THEO: Wait! If you won't take cash...Sebastian. Do you still have that ring? The one I asked you to give to Sylvia?

JULIA: Here it is.

THEO: Okay, kids. This ring is worth a...wait! This isn't the ring I gave you!

JULIA: Oh...sorry. I gave you the wrong ring. Here it...

THEO: But this is the ring I gave Julia! Where did you get this?

JULIA: It was given to me by someone I thought loved me.

THEO: What? Julia gave you this? My Julia? You love my Julia? I'll kill you with my bare hands!

JULIA: No...it wasn't given to me by Julia. It was given to her!

THEO: What?

JULIA: By the only person in the world I love more than Julia. Theo.

(She removes her disguise – which could mean something as simple as taking off her hat and letting her hair down.)

THEO: Julia!

JULIA: Theo!

(They embrace.)

IRVING: Good grief! It's a disease!

(Julia breaks the embrace, steps back, then hauls off and belts Theo.)

JULIA: What is the matter with you?

THEO: Oh, I don't know! I don't blame you for being angry! I don't know what came over me.

JULIA: You're going to have to do better than that!

THEO: No wonder I liked Sebastian so much! Oh, Julia, I see now how wrong I was. I was taken in by Sylvia's shallow glamour...but she's nothing compared to a real girl like you!

SYLVIA: Excuse me! I'm right here!

VAL: Hey! I'm not enough for you?

SYLVIA: *(Giggling:)* More than enough!

VAL: Good, because I like your shallow glamour!

IRVING: This is getting more and more disgusting!

QUEENIE: Seriously!

THEO: Oh, Julia, please forgive me! I'll never stray again...I promise!

JULIA: Well...you did threaten to kill Sebastian when you thought I loved him...

THEO: And I would have! Or beaten him silly, anyway!

JULIA: All right...I'll forgive you. But you're on probation, mister! You'd better stick close!

THEO: Oh, you don't have to worry about that!

(Skip Thurio and Lance, with Crab, burst in, followed by one or more POLICE OFFICERS and Wilma Duke.)

OFFICER: Hands up! You're all under arrest!

WILMA: Hand over my daughter!

LANCE: Sorry, dudes.

VAL: What is this?

SYLVIA: *(Simultaneously:)* Wait! You don't understand!

FRANKY: Coppers!

QUEENIE: Coppers? What movie have you been watching?

FRANKY: Cops, then!

OFFICER: I said hands up!

FRANKY: Are we going to lie down for this, men?

GLORIA: And women!

FRANKY: And women?

STREET KIDS: No!

> *(Another big, comic fight. Wilma, Val, Sylvia, Theo and Julia stand aloof from the fighting, and Lance tries to, but he gets drawn in. When it's over, Two Street Kids are sitting on Skip, the Police Officers stand with Speed "covering" them with one of their own batons, and Lance sits on the ground, nursing unspecific minor wounds.)*

SKIP: You won't get away with this!

WILMA: No, you won't! Officer, I insist you arrest these people! They kidnapped my daughter!

SYLVIA: But I haven't been kidnapped!

WILMA: You haven't?

SKIP: *(Simultaneously:)* You haven't?

SYLVIA: No, of course not!

GLORIA: Wait...yes you have!

FRANKY: *(Elbowing her:)* No, she hasn't.

GLORIA: Right! No, she hasn't.

SYLVIA: I'm here by my own free will...with Val!

WILMA: Val!

OFFICER: Wait a minute! So there's no crime here?

VAL: None whatsoever. Sorry, officer.

OFFICER: *(Disgusted:)* Fine! I'm out of here, then. Come on, men!

(The Officers exit. [Obviously if there is only one, the last sentence can be deleted.] Sylvia crosses to where Skip is still pinned down.)

SYLVIA: Oh, let him up, guys. He's harmless.

(The Street Kids start to let Skip up, but Franky stops them.)

FRANKY: Hold it! I'm in charge here! *(Sheepishly:)* Let him up, guys.

(They do.)

SKIP: I protest! Sylvia, how can you be with this upstart when you could have me?

VAL: Hey!

SYLVIA: Now listen up, Skip. *And* Mother: I love Val. I don't love Skip, or anyone else, and I never will. So you can stop interfering in my life right now!

WILMA: Hey, don't let me stop you.

VAL: What?

SKIP: *(Simultaneously:)* What?

WILMA: Actually, Val, I've been meaning to tell you: I've got a fantastic part for you if you want it.

SKIP: Hey, what about me?

WILMA: Oh, put a sock in it, Skip. You're old hat. They want new blood!

VAL: That's great! But I think I've got something else I want to do first. *(To Sylvia:)* Sylvia...will you marry me? Soon?

SYLVIA: You bet your Equity card!

THEO: *(To Julia:)* What do you say...shall we make it a double wedding?

JULIA: I thought you'd never ask. *(Aside:)* I *really* thought you'd never ask!

SYLVIA: *(To Val:)* Hey! After we're married, what do you say we adopt all these kids?

QUEENIE: Adopt?! What do you mean, adopt?

IRVING: What do you think...we got no parents?

SYLVIA: Well, I just thought...

GLORIA: Please! My Dad's an investment banker!

FRANKY: And my Mom's a Broadway producer!

QUEENIE: We just hang out here for fun.

GLORIA: Keeps us off the streets...well, you know what I mean.

VAL: Well, okay, then!

SKIP: Wait a minute! Where does all this leave me?

STREET KIDS: Oh, put a sock in it, Skip!

LANCE: Relax, dude! Have I got the girl for you!

SKIP: Really?

LANCE: Sure, man. She's a great cook...and I'm sure she'll like you. I'll get you her number.

SPEED: Speaking of cooking, I'm hungry. Come on, Lance. Let's go get something to eat.

LANCE: I know, I know...I'm buying.

WILMA: No, I'm buying. What do you say we all go to Sardi's? *(Looking around at the Street Kids:)* They won't know what hit them!

(Tableau. Blackout. The end.)

The Author Speaks

What inspired you to write this play?
I've always had a soft spot for Shakespeare's *Two Gentlemen of Verona*. It's not one of the bard's "great" masterworks, but it's zany and light and fun. I especially love the character of Launce, and his dog, Crab. I thought it would be fun to treat the play in a contemporary style, while maintaining the ingenious structure of the original.

Was the structure of the play influenced by any other work?
Obviously very much so. I've made plenty of changes in the details, naturally, but structurally the play is a very close adaptation of Shakespeare's play.

Have you dealt with the same theme in other works that you have written?
Not really. At bottom this is essentially a romantic comedy, and I think it's the first one I've written.

What writers have had the most profound effect on your style?
Well, Shakespeare, obviously. But I think I'm more influenced by the playwriting of Oscar Wilde and Eugene Ionesco (yes, I know — an odd combo) and the novels and short stories of P.G. Wodehouse. I'm always more impressed by masterful comedy writing than by more "serious" writers. What the three writers above have in common, for me, is an exquisite sense of comic timing and an unerring instinct for precisely the right word. All three also seem to me to have a wonderful eye and ear for the absurdity of the commonplace.

What are the most common mistakes that occur in productions of your work?
The easiest way to screw up a play like this is to lose the rhythm through overdone transitions. Shakespeare's structure (and mine) is intended to flow immediately from scene to scene, like a film. Ideally, each scene begins the instant the previous one ends. That's why this play is better performed with virtually no scenery — again, as Shakespeare's version would have been. Scene changes are deadly.

What inspired you to become a playwright?
I've been involved in theatre all my life, and I've spent all of my adult life involved in theatre with and for young people. I started writing because there really just isn't a whole lot of really quality material available that's well-suited for performance by young people — that's about things young people care about, with good, juicy roles for young people to play.

Are any characters modeled after real life or historical figures?
Not by me. As far as I know, not by Shakespeare, either. Well, actually, that's not entirely true. Shakespeare gave me the characters of Sylvia and Julia, but their language and personalities do reflect a pair of students I once taught, who were best friends despite being very, very different. I've used them in several plays, actually.

Shakespeare gave advice to the players in *Hamlet*; if you could give advice to your cast what would it be?
Well, I like most of what Hamlet had to say. But he's talking about tragedy. Since this is a comedy, I would also advise my cast to keep it moving. That doesn't mean always talking very fast. It means picking up cues immediately, keeping the ball

rolling. Timing is absolutely critical in comedy. "Dead air" is just that.

About the Author

Matt Buchanan is a New England-based professional playwright and composer specializing in theatre with and for young people. His plays and musicals have been performed across the United States and in several foreign countries. He is also an accomplished stage and music director, as well as a performing musician. He was a founding member of the Boston rock band System Underload. Matt has a BA in Music from Harvard College and an MFA in Child Drama from the University of Texas at Austin.

About YouthPLAYS

YouthPLAYS (www.youthplays.com) is a publisher of award-winning professional dramatists and talented new discoveries, each with an original theatrical voice, and all dedicated to expanding the vocabulary of theatre for young actors and audiences. On our website you'll find one-act and full-length plays and musicals for teen and pre-teen (and even college) actors, as well as duets and monologues for competition. Many of our authors' works have been widely produced at high schools and middle schools, youth theatres and other TYA companies, both amateur and professional, as well as at elementary schools, camps, churches and other institutions serving young audiences and/or actors worldwide. Most are intended for performance by young people, while some are intended for adult actors performing for young audiences.

YouthPLAYS was co-founded by professional playwrights Jonathan Dorf and Ed Shockley. It began merely as an additional outlet to market their own works, which included a substantial body of award-winning published and unpublished plays and musicals. Those interested in their published plays were directed to the respective publishers' websites, and unpublished plays were made available in electronic form. But when they saw the desperate need for material for young actors and audiences—coupled with their experience that numerous quality plays for young people weren't finding a home—they made the decision to represent the work of other playwrights as well. Dozens and dozens of authors are now members of the YouthPLAYS family, with scripts available both electronically and in traditional acting editions. We continue to grow as we look for exciting and challenging plays and musicals for young actors and audiences.

About ProduceaPlay.com

Let's put up a play! Great idea! But producing a play takes time, energy and knowledge. While finding the necessary time and energy is up to you, ProduceaPlay.com is a website designed to assist you with that third element: knowledge.

Created by YouthPLAYS' co-founders, Jonathan Dorf and Ed Shockley, ProduceaPlay.com serves as a resource for producers at all levels as it addresses the many facets of production. As Dorf and Shockley speak from their years of experience (as playwrights, producers, directors and more), they are joined by a group of award-winning theatre professionals and experienced teachers from the world of academic theatre, all making their expertise available for free in the hope of helping this and future generations of producers, whether it's at the school or university level, or in community or professional theatres.

The site is organized into a series of major topics, each of which has its own page that delves into the subject in detail, offering suggestions and links for further information. For example, Publicity covers everything from Publicizing Auditions to How to Use Social Media to Posters to whether it's worth hiring a publicist. Casting details Where to Find the Actors, How to Evaluate a Resume, Callbacks and even Dealing with Problem Actors. You'll find guidance on your Production Timeline, The Theater Space, Picking a Play, Budget, Contracts, Rehearsing the Play, The Program, House Management, Backstage, and many other important subjects.

The site is constantly under construction, so visit often for the latest insights on play producing, and let it help make your play production dreams a reality.

Also from YouthPLAYS

The Unscary Ghost by Matt Buchanan
Comedy. 40-50 minutes. 3+ males, 5+ females (13-30+ performers possible).

Loosely based on Oscar Wilde's *The Canterville Ghost.* When the Otis family moves into the old Victorian home in Canterville, Ohio, they soon learn that the place is haunted— by a ghost who can't scare anyone. The jaded, modern family alternately taunts and tries to exploit the unfortunate ghost, Simon Canter, even trying to get a spot on the hit TV show, *America's Most Haunted.* Only the oldest daughter, Ginny, seems to care for or understand poor Simon. Can she help him find peace? A sometimes zany, sometimes touching show for the whole family.

Sidekickin' It! by Adam J. Goldberg
Comedy. 23-30 minutes. 2 females, 6-9 either (8-11 performers possible).

The story of Robin, a precocious girl with gumption beyond her years, and Daybreak, a superhero who finds he will need more than the ability to lift really, really heavy stuff if he is going to stop humanity's destruction at the hands of the diabolical Von Darkness. Watch Robin teach Daybreak that no power is greater than the power of friendship.

Twinkle Toes by Bradley Hayward
Dramedy. 30-35 minutes. 3 males, 3 females.

Calvin, a flamboyant high school senior, prepares for the most important day of his life. As his audition for the Julliard School of Dance approaches, he spends day and night on the dance floor. His friends and family rally at his side, but he has a broken heart that must be mended before he can stand on tiptoe and take his place in the spotlight.

The Bread, the Bracelet, and the Dove by Claudia Haas

Comedy. 40-50 minutes. 2 males, 10-16 females, 6 either (12-24 performers possible).

Based on an Italian folktale, the play centers around what Italians love best: food and family. Amid an array of colorful, quirky, emotional characters, two children save a magical dove and learn up close and personal about the meaning of famiglia. Set in a lively marketplace in Renaissance Italy, the play is fast-paced, lively, with moments of great silliness and sweetness.

The Butterfly: Legends from the Middle Kingdom by Ruth Cantrell

Young Audiences. 50-55 minutes. 2-4 males, 2-4 females (5-6 performers possible).

Chou, an innocent child born in prison, is befriended by a yellow butterfly that has the ability to bring stories to life. The stories, from Chinese folklore and the Beijing opera, transport Chou and others to various places in the middle kingdom. Such a valuable creature would bring wealth to its owner, and the other prisoners and guards attempt to steal the yellow butterfly. Chou warns the butterfly to flee, but it tells one last story…

Masks by Paul E. Doniger

Comedy. 100-120 minutes. 5 males, 6 females, 2 either and 6-12+ extras (19-40 performers possible).

A poignant and hilarious love story set in a struggling Commedia troupe. Young Pierette replaces her father in the comic performances, then nearly destroys the company by falling in love with the faithless Flavio. The mix of classic dell'Arte performances and the dramatic lives of the offstage actors creates a completely unique theatrical experience with challenging roles for all of the performers.

Made in the USA
San Bernardino, CA
27 September 2014